FORGE

FORGE

POEMS BY

TED MATHYS

COFFEE HOUSE PRESS

MINNEAPOLIS

2005

Coffee House Press books are available to the trade through our primary distributor, Consortium Book Sales & Distribution, 1045 Westgate Drive, Saint Paul, MN 55114. For personal orders, catalogs, or other information, write to: Coffee House Press, 27 North Fourth Street, Suite 400, Minneapolis, MN 55401.

Coffee House Press is a nonprofit literary publishing house. Support from private foundations, corporate giving programs, government programs, and generous individuals help make the publication of our books possible. We gratefully acknowledge their support in detail in the back of this book.

Good books are brewing at coffeehousepress.org

LIBRARY OF CONGRESS CATALOGING-IN-PUBLICATION DATA

Mathys, Ted, 1979–
Forge / Ted Mathys.
p. cm.
ISBN-13: 978-1-56689-178-3 (alk. paper)
ISBN-10: 1-56689-178-7 (alk. paper)
1. Ohio—Poetry. 2. New York (N.Y.)—Poetry.
3. Europe, Eastern—Poetry.
I. Title.
PS3613.A829F67 2005
811'.6—dc22
2005012804

FIRST EDITION | FIRST PRINTING
1 3 5 7 9 8 6 4 2
Printed in the United States

CONTENTS

Built that They May Find Their Tongues   1

FACTORIES

Humming in the Factory of Yesness   5

The Factory of Liquid Is a Lair   7

Inventory   8

Cherries in the Factory of Blackness   10

A Whole in the Factory of Null   12

Inventory   14

The Factory in the Factory of Simultaneity   15

Paused in the Factory of Choice   18

Inventory   20

The Factory of What I Loved   21

**A LITTLE RELIGION OF
SLEDGEHAMMERS AND MANDARINS**

Meanwhile the Grove Tree   25

Or Am I Buried Up to My Throat Only to Coax   26

Nor the Artist   27

That Moment Back   28

Then the Synesthetes   29

Only to Ding   30

Not So Much that She Wakes   31

In Hunter's   32

Otherwise the Dollhouse   33

The Demolition   34

Amiss   35

However the Object   36

THE HOLE IN THE FOG   41

CONCUSSION

Ailment   59

Ash Wednesday   61

Hemispheres   65

Mekong, Mohican   67

Spun   70

Lucian through an Achromatic Lens   73

Junk Suite   74

QUANDARIES   81

ACKNOWLEDGMENTS

Grateful acknowledgment is made to the editors of the following publications, in which these poems, or versions thereof, first appeared:

Aufgabe:	from "Quandaries"
Black Warrior Review:	"Built that They May Find Their Tongues"
	"Junk Suite"
The Canary:	"A Whole in the Factory of Null"
	"The Factory of Liquid Is a Lair"
Chelsea:	"The Hole in the Fog"
Colorado Review:	"Paused in the Factory of Choice"
Fence:	"Meanwhile the Grove Tree"
	"Nor the Artist"
	"Then the Synesthetes"
Forklift, Ohio:	"Inventory" [p. 14]
Good Foot:	"Not So Much that She Wakes"
	"Otherwise the Dollhouse"
Gulf Coast:	"Inventory" [p. 20]
Indiana Review:	"Hemispheres"
jubilat:	"The Factory of What I Loved"
LIT:	"The Demolition"
Mid-American Review:	"Mekong, Mohican"
MiPoesias (www.mipoesias.com):	"Cherries in the Factory of Blackness"
	"However the Object"
Ploughshares:	"Humming in the Factory of Yesness"
Rogue Scholars Collective (www.roguescholarscollective.com):	"Spun"

Swerve: "In Hunter's"

                                     "Lucian through an Achromatic
                                     Lens"

                                     "Only to Ding"

                                     "That Moment Back"

Verse: "Ailment"

                                     "Or Am I Buried Up to My Throat
                                     Only to Coax"

                                     "The Factory in the Factory of
                                     Simultaneity"

Verse Blog
(versemag.blogspot.com):   "Ash Wednesday"

Web Conjunctions
(www.conjunctions.com):   from "Quandaries"

"Inventory" [p. 20] was reprinted as a limited edition broadside by
The Center for Book Arts, designed and printed by Julia Benjamin
and Ana Cordeiro.

Many thanks to my family and friends for their support. Thanks to
those who provided suggestions and comments on this work: Brian
Engel-Fuentes, Sarah Fox, Ben Lerner, Timothy Liu, Chris Martin,
Bree Nordenson, Nick Rattner, Fred Schmalz, Madeleine Marie
Slavick, Leah Wiste, and Zheng Danyi. Thank you Bob Holman and
Elizabeth Murray. Thanks to Chris Fischbach and everyone at Coffee
House Press. Impossibly, thank you Greg Hewett, mentor, collabora-
tor, poet in the spheres.

FORGE

BUILT THAT THEY MAY FIND THEIR TONGUES

They built a lamb and started with the hooves.
They affixed some legwork, the lamb resembled a shrub.
They made the torso a lattice of tissue and remorse.
The lamb trotted off toward a deep reservoir.
Lamb ran with pronation, some followed with ointment.
They were drawn to the depth, drew cards from a deck.
The cards were all spades so they dug deeper still.
They spent hours with the lamb bluffing on a cliff.
Threw feathers into gulches and waited for an echo.
Disregarded horses and slipped into dark waters.
Asked history to absolve them, those echoes to come.
To the lamb they gave troubled allegiance and grass.
They fell in love with the concepts of love and cud.
Lamb masticated grass so it would not vomit.
Lamb swallowed allegiance when they wanted it back.
The lamb was urgent, the lamb was necessity.
They built a lamb and it could not speak.
The lamb walked on stilts and restricted their sleep.
They loved the lamb and it asked to be worshipped.
They worshipped the lamb and it asked to be offed.
The lamb was patient as they set it on the pyre.
The lamb just kept dying over and over.
As their fathers built cement foundations.
As their mothers built theories and verbs.
As fields of ragweed were condemned.

As their lamb could not speak a word.
Their lamb is not theirs it has made that clear.
They built a lamb then the lamb built them.
How the lamb then struggled with impossible vocables:
"ul"   "iieu"   "loah"
They built a lamb and they shaved it raw.
The wool was fibrous, the fibers were hollow.
They stuck splinters of thought inside the fibers.
They knitted the lamb a sweater of itself.   "float. float."
The lamb never grew, the lamb only lambed.
The problem of the lamb was the problem of a name.
One named it Paradox for its dichotomous mind.
The lamb was in motion but its motions were motionless.
One named it Pandora and their curiosities were large.
They put the lamb in a vessel in a vessel in a vessel.
One named it Poem and again it went animal.
Their lamb fanatical, the fanatic an oracle.
Lamb busting out of vessel out of vessel out of vessel.
A seeing-eye lamb and they were the blind.
The delicate beast dragged them around by a harness.
Who had trained the lamb to avoid such traffic?
Who had fashioned all these previous hooves?
The lamb brought back news from unreachable pastures.
The lamb excavated black-eyed Susans and unseens.
The lamb boxed them in with a solid blue gaze.
They gave the lamb hands and the lamb said
            "make."

FACTORIES

HUMMING IN THE
FACTORY OF YESNESS

So there goes the whole note, the soprano's
nonexistent solo; the color of a dye otherwise
known as cyan; there goes the last instant, wait
for the next; remember a set of thumbs
gesturing like suffocating bluegill on a gig-line; here goes
the *sotto voce,* the vulgar aside; i before e
except ceiling fans everywhere and terrifying;
remember the bathrobe and how mungy she looked;
all this muchness, all this heft; there goes the finger-sex,
constant as a tractor beam in the glove of the woods;
small dogs in sweaters will sniff and suppose,
sniff and remember; the next instant comes
and we are unimpressed;
there goes a cheap dojo, a rictus grin;
remember the visible dimples in the canvas, the statues
that lob and possess, lob and possess
better shadows than us; there goes a wet horse
into the scabbard of sleep; "can't run a tab here, no dice—
Miller in a mason jar, Miller Lite in a can";
remember the birch with their alabaster skin,
the aphids in the oaks, their little pillows of death;
remember the sledge into the skull of the cow,
the flannel that swung it; allergic to butter, dust, and trees,
where to go now; all this otherwise, all this taupe;
there goes the light switch, who turned on the fan;

still the small dogs in their sweaters on their four feet,
lithe; remember the pastor, his ermine smile;
most crossroads don't cross but merge and branch
and nobody ever stands at them;
"Miller in a mason jar, Miller Lite in a can";
there goes the evidence, the big-ass limn;
leggy, holding it in, one more, baby, "uno";
as her hair curls like a wound
heals, red and effortlessly

THE FACTORY OF LIQUID
IS A LAIR

As rain alone has the gall to wipe out the sun,
hanging there like a cyst on the firmament;
as dew presses into a cluster of acacia leaves,
into a timid mimosa that closes when touched;
as *evanesce* could be a direction, as *sublimate* a plot;
"now that I've traced small hearts with your semen
on your rib cage I want you to meet my parents";
in which vapor pressure builds, roiling cogwheels in the skull;
as her blood on the sheets turns umber by morning,
before bleach wipes it out like the sun the dew;
as dew knows the temperature of its own conception
and looms at that threshold like an arrow cocked in oxbow;
as milk will congeal in the stomach, if it's only given time;
"that dude can do shit with stringy saliva like blow
bubbles on his lips or gurney it down then suck it back up";
in which a mooring buoy is anchored, to mark the site of loss;
as choir boys invade silence with silky canticles,
their robes rippling reflections on deeper bodies of water;
as a head of foam hovers on the surface of the lager
like a ghost or constellation in the shape of lower Asia;
as cascading begins in the urinals, and the ? turns its head;
"the swamp already smells skanky, that's why Mom
wastes skunks with her shotgun in the elms";
the factory in which each palette of want stacked
splashes then scatters across the loading-dock floor;
in which the guileless frolic and the gill-less drown

INVENTORY

Box springs plus mattress where we barely slept
together, storm-torn of our scent, exposed
black coils, abandoned, a rib cage
on a drift of snow; three cinder blocks stacked
in a miniature plinth, absent of statuary,
as if their sole purpose was to buttress
the time of our singing or the ceiling of the sky;
between two skylights, a steel ladder fastened
with ladder jacks, empty rungs up the slope
of a wet slate roof, no one ascending
toward the wet crow at the peak, pacing;
an abandoned wok, silver and overturned
at the base of the air shaft like an ear to the ground;
the first story I couldn't remember, the second story I had to forget;
the wooden spoon beside me, ovular and still
in the shape of your face; the wet crow appears
to be staring at me, I appear to be staring back,
there does not appear an exit, no escape;
only the coolness of this wrought-iron fire-
escape railing, alone with its shadows, its angular blue;
screw these fingernails, too damn healthy; a phalanx
of matchsticks stuck in the flowerpot; the daddy
longlegs drinking from a puddle of milk;
how each escape seems merely wrought; the former
iron and fire hovering somewhere above *the first
story I couldn't remember, the second story I had to forget;*

while on the third-story ledge our suicidal cat, no more, no
less suicidal than when you left, still bats his scabbed
boxer paws toward an invisible canary beyond

CHERRIES IN THE FACTORY
OF BLACKNESS

Even where the cherry emits the only
glow; "can I bum a smoke" and I
love you like an alibi; over the Sterno
a marshmallow on a pitchfork blackens;
where the absence of the sparkling is an earring
adored yet neglected in a tackle box, a snelled
fishhook threaded through her lobe in lieu
of the perfectly compassed silver hoop;
even where security in the dim is a form
of barking through dulled molars;
according to the plummet, according to the dark;
of course a power outage then the tyranny
of the fuse box; near the wick of the lambent
candle on the table a parabola of blue-
blackness inside light inside black-
blueness; close the eyes and squeal;
even where deeper registers of color
locate deeper registers of sound; the neurotic
wail of an unseen killdeer, a man leaning
into formica to order the appetizer
"bluebirds over bullet wounds";
the moss-rot smell of indigo space;
according to the plummet, according to the dark;
even where water alone refuses its own
claustrophobia and every memento

is a form of onyx; the stoic bronze monkey
on the platter's all shadows and balances
a basket of black opium on his head;
chase the dragon, close the eyes;
look, the hood torn off at dusk to run
screaming through the cherry trees;
even where at this color and hour you remove
your sadness, fold it in thirds, and place it
at the foot of the mattress to keep
warm for wearing in better light

A WHOLE IN THE FACTORY OF NULL

Sure before the invention of zero the shepherd didn't have zero
sheeps the shepherd had "this many sheeps" the shepherd
said while not raising his opposing
thumbs; so which speared bullfrog
is about to hack its last phlegmatic cough
under the unashamed espionage of the sun;
how a red kayak executes a barrel roll over
water moccasins; how everything is destroyed when divided
by *nothing*; pluck a willow branch to locate a concubine;
"Moses had a baby and its head popped off";
how having made varsity in pathos and with all these intimacy
issues he simply needed to be a porcupine;
overturn the empty, overturn *what if*;
sure there are those who read the last
page first and those of us who don't
read it at all; so the eighth chakra is apparently this aura;
"Atlas held a heaven and its head popped off";
how this loaf of sourdough smells
like sex and sure that sells; so let me rub
a dandelion under your chin and if
you turn yellow you like butter; no we're not
exactly naked and null, this is fishnet these are chains;
sure there is chatter in the grammar of numbers, in the logic of wind;
to measure the floorboards sling me an abacus;
so he wasn't being clever when he said the saw blade *sings*;

diamond-tipped, RPM; to frame the gable, call
me the angle, the bevel, the degree, and you know Christ
was a carp; "History had a baby and its head popped off";
overturn the empty, overturn *what if;*
where the question becomes how to regurgitate straight
into the mouth of your gift horse held
open like a zero, like the calcium curtain to a show
nobody wants to watch

INVENTORY

Jumbo eggs, four pennies, unjellied
toast, spork minus prong, one staunch
red pepper, spiral notebook, no pen, ropes of rain
braiding out the window, bowl of beans (black and kidney)
over risotto, small box turtle called Gus (head retracted,
tweaking out), granules of salt, my hands amok
with anxiety and butter, an unedited letter
to the Marquis de Sade I found in your sock
drawer & held onto, loose tea, immediacy, conquistador
on the nook poster, my unedited letter
to Freud which begins *Dear Sigmund,*
my id is a slum for comparison, a dried-out calla lily
flaccid as molted snakeskin, a memory of the single
raised freckle behind your ear, extra salt and an extra spork
though I'm certain you won't show up,
four lengths of rope in case you do

THE FACTORY IN THE FACTORY OF SIMULTANEITY

A white rocket ship exits Atari screen right,
enters left, kills stuff, exits right,
enters left; a cashier cracks a roll of quarters
on the register drawer; under the shower head
a boy momentarily forgets his recurring dream of _____;
"The end zone's soaked and damn if it ain't still
raining like a cow pissing on a flat rock";
if the new physics is right, the universe is not
endless void but concentric donuts interwoven, starlight
is the original blip-rocket, always observing the back of its own
bright nape and most of these stars are
reflections of a few, their flicker, simultaneously not *here;*
"Where Tammy at"; a seventeen-year locust
approaches the surface, a furnace clicks, a cistern
explodes; we are all at all times either
making love or not making love;
even pinstripes manage to coexist;
photograph of guitar, sickle, bandolier; the weight of her hair
in the little silk pouch, the dark bulge of her calf
where the leech sleeps; a towering house of cards
the moment before collapse;
"Hi Dave this is Patty I finally
got the new electric wheelchair and a venereal please call me
I really need to talk to you"; a sparrow
suffocates in a tub of honey;

she paints her roommate's pinky
fingernail teal with a gold
racing stripe as talisman;
here is transcription of synchronicity, *there* it exists, indigo, is
a shovel propped up between opposite
mirrors, exponential; the silkworm
could be equal to provolone, the i-beam
equal to the cornea, the pool cue equal to gun turret,
elephant mask to scream; astral projection and lean;
time a color only seen by insects, a sound only heard by hounds;
"Calm the fuck down, man, I'll be your yenta";
the waitress realigns the banana
clip in her hair like an antenna to new
frequencies; at once,
a worker stirs a fiberglass vat of grain with her boot
and remembers her mother's bound feet, deep plum;
"That baby's toes was long as a seven-penny nail and thicker";
in the painting the impasto daubs of red are regarded
together as a coherent nosebleed; each punk band can
wail with just guitar sprain, mullets, and the truth, but
inside language can a hand be simultaneously
thumbing the incunabula and becoming
crimson with paper cuts; neither the either/or nor the neither/nor;
drop the needles onto dual
turntables for layers of one voice
imitating itself above, below, *there;* a science fair
project charting the flow of a bucket of water
dumped in the Gulf, appearing in Shanghai;
read it left to right, top to bottom; but does dancing require time;

an arboreal shadow mimics its limb; "bog roll, podunk, fuzz";
not the mere resurrection of *other,* but the distance
between *other* and *or the;* "oh, the
sharpest one you got, I suppose"; *there*
the body habitually wanting to press into both
the greater and lesser surfaces; the body as
bunions & marrow & the shape of things touched,
& not the body blank, not an asymptote or palimpsest,
but the body to be and not to be, with fur on the tongue

PAUSED IN THE FACTORY OF CHOICE

Kiss the scoop of your lover's unpredictable clavicle or
kiss the wet nose of a foal, still, one hoof raised, ready
to bolt; ignite a riotous August bonfire
in the soybean field, standing so far back
from the blast of heat and light whose plume of smoke and ash
flails like a busy quill above a curlicue of sparks
going cobalt to apricot to black
that you get cold, or kindle
a quiet fire compassed only by stones,
huddle close, stay low, keep warm;
"you can bang on the solenoid if you got a good hammer
or just get a new starter but it'll cost you like shit";
be a shadow or that which casts it;
have the quiet afterlife of a black iris
or the quiet afterlife of a black handgun;
"one-one-thousand, two-Mississippi, three-one-thousand,
four-Mississippi, five-one-thousand, six-Mississippi, ollie ollie
oxen freeee"; achieve neurosis in the manner of sycamore branches
or in the manner of 1923; have the arteries of Kahlo
and the boils of Marx or the dreams of Dali
and the death of Marat; have an alibi or none;
"pretty soon, Aaron, you're gonna have to make some decisions";
kill a tree or a salamander; kill a mood or a goat;
count your poems, count your money; count yourself;
save a stamp or a scab, save a coin or generation;

catch the ball, catch the breeze, catch the bullhead;

carve a pumpkin or yourself, carve a name or yourself;

count the firewood, would you rather, count the hatchets, would you rather;

catch the moment, find your tongue, catch the snow, watch it flame

INVENTORY

An argument of sirens, one twitching pigeon
on the nose of the stoic stone lion, two more
like sentries flanking the roman numeral carved
into the portico's marble frontispiece:

      pigeon, MDCCCXCV, *pigeon,*

a security guard at the entrance inspecting bags
for bombs, a security guard at the exit inspecting bags
for books, the vaulted stone ceiling, three flights of echo
to the Rose Reading Room, quiet as an ice floe,
one-hundred-seventy-two bronze-shaded lamps bolted four
to a table, all on, some in use, that one by a lone
cirrhotic scholar with quick wrists and a bloodshot eye,
at table position five-hundred-fifty-nine a teal-bound
edition of *Come Hither* compiled by Walter de la Mare
you would have liked, four electrical outlets, two screws,
a brass plate, and my blanched skin still smelling
chemical because this morning, after you bolted,
I was on my knees between the bed and the wall, scrubbing
away at the scripture of boot marks you left on the paint,
illegible calligraphy your feet wrote as you writhed, as you drew
a little penumbra of blood from my shoulder, your dark echo writ
large as this reading room's, because it required more
than an hour to remove, because I began with Windex
and a ripped, white v-neck T-shirt,
because I wanted to scrub forever,
because I had to resort to bleach

THE FACTORY OF
WHAT I LOVED

The Sawzall and pocket hole, the tin snips and J-channel,
the lauan and the hammer, and the wrist; I spent
most free time on benches, freely absorbing
the pain of others; the mentioned and the century,
the rag and the king, the quilt and the helix,
and the wrist; I spit and somewhere the barn swallows
gather in a hayloft, their eyes burning like anthracite—
all heat, no smoke, no flame; is to be so thermal
to reconstitute the grounds for hope; *to give heat
is within the control of every human being;*
all the uncles uncomfortable in their skein of being
creatures of the so and so and with songs; "Angel Face, Angel Face,
eyes so bloo, come on over here so I can make love to you";
the trowel and the poured core, the rebar and the level,
the wine and the knife, and the wrist; "Nappy Head, Nappy Head,
eyes like a frog, roll yo ass over so I can slay you like a dog";
inertia spits and somewhere the chimney swallows
hurl into brick, wings slap soot, as if hope
were sidelong, this pliant; the anima and the animus,
the public and the quark, the dream and the lack,
and the wrist, the wrist

A LITTLE RELIGION OF SLEDGEHAMMERS AND MANDARINS

MEANWHILE THE GROVE TREE

sweats baby mandarins. Middle branches, just beyond the approaching hand. Among them recur one or two of obscene glamour. The rest appear no more lucent than noodle-shop Formica. Be patient, be a member of the hesitant. They will gather up in late summer's humid belly and rot. They will drop and not bounce. Pick up one that is crow-black. Carry it as talisman.

OR AM I BURIED UP TO MY THROAT ONLY TO COAX

you, sun, into loving me again? Sand is assembling in my eyes. Your swirling sky over the coast is a boatload of paella. I've come to share communion wine but remain splayed by bop-apocryphal hues. See the sea's horizon as your quilt. Lift your veil as you sink. I'll scatter you with pebbles. Launch your bouquet of red glaze. I'll write hieroglyphs in dunes. I have met the overlooked thieves of Golgotha and they spoke of sand. So here I am, bivouacked in it. A beach runt. Others have called out to you from the trenches of their own unfortunate beaches, but this plot is mine, sun, and I vote to straddle it as you set. I vote for the globe's inevitable somersault back into blackness, as black refuses shadows. Except for the time at the collection when the one called Goya disemboweled me with *The Forge* and its three peasant men beating sledges into molten iron. All else folded into impossible shades of black across the canvas, but I got distracted and started tailing the Italian-looking woman with tight pants across the gallery. Because I was practicing love at first sight. Then in a certain *Deposition* Christ's limp face frozen in pale terra-cotta made me care a little less about her heron chin and sexy knees. But when staring at the Lord's flayed wrist being kissed by those deposing I felt her breath on my neck, only then did I know I would not be forgiven.

NOR THE ARTIST

bloated with the knowledge that things were growing at the tissue
level of organization. That the skin-bag without strangled fruit
trees within. Seventeenth century: calligraphy: shamming deaf-
ness and pauperism at the end of the Ming he slung his freshly
bladed testicles at a sheet of rice paper. Titled the painting
Pomegranates. Copious blood flow onto a dirt floor brings a slow
throb similar to sleepwalking. Somnambulant, he pulled from his
pocket a black mandarin.

THAT MOMENT BACK

in the center of the night, in the center of the state, in an acre of fierce alfalfa when you were slamming me like a sledgehammer a tack, there among the furrows infused with zinc oxide for the coming lightning storm. The crickets were in an uproar so you tore off your shirt and in lieu of your left breast was a gaping cavity through which I could see Orion's thigh, and his sword was raised too, imagine that, and we both knew that the aftermath of downpour could soon siphon an entire regiment of night crawlers up through the soil where they might animate our legs and writhe like hydra over our heads, and who doesn't fear Medusas? So I plunged my arm through the dark lacuna in your chest, up to my elbow, and patted you on the back, saying *there there dogchild*, and then pulled you in closer, and closer still.

THEN THE SYNESTHETES

agreed. How sour the rhombus, how scarlet the vowel. The func-
tion proceeded as planned. Rimbaud demanded derangement
and fairy juice, Kandinsky and Liszt tasted a plate of chords and
strokes, Gorky in the corner in a beanie heard the echo of apri-
cots and unleavened bread, Nabokov lurched open the oak
door—who invited Rilke? Rilke: *Dance the Orange*... and blessed
be the semicircle, for when the music went linear, the party
formed a sickle. Danced for the black mandarin on the floor like
eunuchs for an emperor.

ONLY TO DING

the vaulted bell at the county fair, I ogre-swung a jumbo sledge at the rubber nugget and made it to *wimp.* At some point I achieved *tough guy,* but never *stud* or *Hercules,* and one day I'll likely die still *tough guy,* because after a certain threshold strength matters less than technique—consider the graceful way plane trees croak. In love with the texture of slick pine, I am given to choking way up on the handle, strangling the neck of sledge more appealing than *stud.* Ultimately resigned, I lope to the arena of rubber frogs, produce a dollar, and load three frogs on my catapult at once. With one deft plunk of the mallet, I send them up into the humidity above the amoebic plastic lilies. When they hover at the apex, wet legs glittering in the sun, I get incredibly sad and think this is what it must be like when a widower spills the urn, and the ashes flutter up like colorless butterflies.

NOT SO MUCH THAT
SHE WAKES

still strapped to the cot. Or that three paramedics lie languorous as moss about the sterile interior of the ambulance. Or even that in this clean dimension of twisted metallics and limbs, she can see clearly through the open door the splinters of the telephone pole beginning to kindle. Not so much that the bluelight veins of flame tease the pole with such simple complexity that she unbites her lip and whispers

abacus

or even that all the windsong and whiskey in the world can't choke out the doubt. But mostly that at this moment she finds herself behind her eyes. She is previous. She floats sideways past the gauze and slinks up the wall. Top shelf. Iodine. Disposables. She sees her hand below. It opens and closes around the dim mandarin. Slowly as the siren, slowly like a valve.

IN HUNTER'S

orange hat and solid Stihl suspenders, my father has decided to paint the blade of his favorite shovel hunter's orange and lop off its tip with a silicon carbide industrial grinder in a blaze of sparks in order to skim soil better. But when he does, it is just too perfect and he cannot let it go, never lets it go. The men begin to call him Linus as he begins to spray-paint sledgehammers, mortar mixers, dike pliers, truck tires, all his fingers, all his mornings, his entire maw, hunter's orange. It is all over the place and I don't know whether it is talisman or addiction, all I can remember are the sparks. I'm behind the silo gouging my fingers into soil in search of buried arrowheads, but when I see his hunter's orange form approaching me like a zombie, dragging his shovel slowly across the shop's concrete floor, I know that perfection is exactly what we have always feared. From the tiny pile of what's been collected, I select two slivers of imperfect flint, lean back and smack them together to launch an orange spark that hovers like the lodestar, pulling everything directionless, while somewhere between us the tomahawks have begun.

OTHERWISE THE DOLLHOUSE

quivers and sings appropriately. Her hand arranges a rocking chair
in the dining room. Little man's trousers are removed, little man
wrapped in a shroud of ceremonial duct tape. Hand wipes peanut
butter on the ceiling of the foyer. Hand thinks. Little man placed
in the kitchen, in the sink, in the disposer. Hand wants electricity,
something fibrous. She retracts hand from rear wall. Rear wall is
filleted open like a mackerel on ice in Macau, heart still beating.
Proof of life. Hand notices little man removing ceremonial duct
tape. Climbing out of the sink. Hand watches man move straight-
legged to the bedroom, pull a black mandarin from beneath the
duvet. Beating.

THE DEMOLITION

Derby requires that the car be stripped of glass, have a governor on the motor, pyrotechnic tailpipe, dolled-up with duct tape, racing stripe, dice on the dash, lucky number, flame retardant, and driver equipped with helmet and conception of history as the pagan saga of sex and warfare. The difference between those two being nearly negligible: see Hector's battle gear shine like a magnesium fire, see him bludgeon a Greek then lick his scarlet finger like a Blow Pop, see Russ in boots heaving a sledge into the windshield to prepare his derby car, see us grunt and sweat as we swing, hear the plash of shattering glass, hear a deep-throated laugh, see Rome and in it a slave fucking Nero with her hand around his swollen throat, see us take it too far, swinging at the tires, the fenders, doors, roof, off in the distance see the saliva gathering in the corner of how many mouths, see the diorama of plastic paratroopers strewn across the pasture and the boy trotting off toward the woods, see the man behind the wheel of a functioning car ask if I could maybe fulfill a high-school fantasy then look crotchward and say "take it out," see the protester insert the long stem of a daisy into the barrel of the Marine's rifle, hear the announcer announcing the derby lineup, whiff the raw funk of goat and funnel cake, see us not present at the grandstand's arena of wetted dirt, see us still in the scrambled field of noxious weeds, swinging our heavy pendulums, see the body of the car, see the body battered, see the body, tear it down.

AMISS

in the rise, the pause, the fall. Stacked in the gut of the abandoned rowboat, a peck of mandarins with eight-ball skin. Not to be asked questions. Not to foresee futures. Never to estimate waves or be exhumed. Pure color loses consequence when viewed in bulk. Supersaturates the retina, though no retina is present. Rise, pause, fall. *Bail the boat gently* says a handwritten note, taped to the left oar. As if the only art to sinking were speed.

HOWEVER THE OBJECT

has become the religion. All former manner of worship dismantled. The rotted black mandarin as seraphim, a sledgehammer on the altar. God notwithstanding, God netting himself hammock-like around antediluvian tools, all over ancient fruits, into the negative space that shapes them. Middle English *slegge,* from Old English *slecg;* akin to Old Norse *sleggja,*—more at SLAY. *Citrus reticulata,* the wings are charred yet the interior retains its born color.

Tonight, activity over the Caribbean. A storm of sledges falling sky to wave, steelhead-heavy like pelicans dive-bombing for mullet. Slender hickory handles whiffling like tail feathers. This is, of course, all nonsense to the disengaged. It may in fact be virtuous to disengage.

At communion I used to get literal with the wafer pressed to my tongue. So this is the taste of human flesh. So this is the stringy musculature of Christ's left thigh. So this is the sweet salt of blood. Beyond actualizing the vine, how else to taste an otherwise inedible god?

As the hammers splash covertly into water, a mandarin on the beach inverts itself. This is no small spherical feat. Black core, orange viscera sandy in the wind. What does it mean, really, to *die of exposure?*

"Then said they unto him, 'What shall we do unto thee, that the sea may be calm unto us?'"

In response I requested to be banished to the tossing water. Instead I got nothing but the blinking of plankton, some luminescence. I'm unable to grasp this as punishment—plankton possesses the godliness these objects ceaselessly sought. All spicule and yolk sac, lucent in the surf. I dunk my fingers in the spume. I stand and place two small seashells over my eyes. There, a frenzied old Norse berserker wanders through the mangroves, humming as he plucks mandarins from the trees then clobbers them with his thunder club. Is this, perhaps, rapture?

To the beach on my right, the inverted mandarin. In front of my feet, a washed-up sledge lathered with seaweed. Though there is no such thing as true repetition, the sea too seems a fugue, wearily riffing on itself.

THE HOLE IN THE FOG

Before rattles
there were riddles

Before riddles
there were gourds

As the riddles
turned to fog

The gourds
dried to rattles

I stood on a rock
and shook them at the sea

*

Ace the footbridge over the Danube to the edge
of the island where the island cleaves

the river and the eddies and water knots
become a horse. The streetlamp's lunar orange

draws moths, hooves
clop, clouds
slump

Who launched the paper
sailboat past the grillwork? *b   bo   boa   boat   oat   at   t*

In the Iliadic cloud low over Parliament, a minor
archer being speared in the liver, crashing from chariot.

The city's edges rough-hewn by mist, there is
something quite wrong with this realism.

We've been warned not to mention totemic animals.

> say "the long-tailed one"
> say "the large-antlered one"
> say "that was not a crow"

*

Switzerland: toward a scrum of orderlies in greens on smoke
break you follow a retinue of sequins dropped on the sidewalk
by nobody. Budapest: I hammer watered-down whiskey and try
writing about wishing you luck. Switzerland: sign, initial,
sign, initial, they roll your body in on the dolly.
Budapest: I throw virgins into volcanoes, good luck.
I put my patience on layaway, good luck. Switzerland:
orderlies pussyfoot through music and put on gloves.
Budapest: the breaker of stallions appears in the cloud.
I fear shields, for you, spears, you, anything in pill form.

*

The river slides through the black
bed of its own making. Point to point

with apparent purpose, but where cut
by the boulder, rapids become a white horseshoe.

Flux, transfer, yet the roan
river remains static on the map. Grass spears

appear as one in the word "lawn" but beneath
the head, individual needles jab jab jab.

There is always movement between points
and there is always movement within the point.

Here, fog operates on principles
of supply and demand—

when nothing external enters to distort

the reality of experience, the reality of experience

distorts itself.

*

The anesthetist led you to the island of Thanatos
from which you did not return. We still hold you

there on the blasted-white beach in your blue
equilateral of hospital cot, water and sky, the i.v. sack

slow over your head like a bubble with the primeval
password: "pulse." Minimalist,

you had called yourself in a huff,
and have now achieved it on sand.

To communicate from your cypress-edged dimension
to mine, you sent a postcard to the waiting

room between us. No postage. In a peripheral
realm a ream of graph paper folded in

upon itself. Coils uncoiled.
I could touch your sternum

and bring in the tide. Who then would have expected
you to wake to your dead dog in der Schweiz

without explanation leaping in through the ward window
in an Alpine cape to lap your face and speak

in tongues that were no tongues at all but the equality
that all tongues take on when you find yourself

in the hole in the fog? The dead retriever is freed
from the fact that he is a dog and that he is dead.

He carefully delineates your purpose as a piece
of both flesh and art in some ecstatic ekphrastic

manner of slobber and vowels. Of course
we understood that when the dog bound

back out into the symmetry of rock and snow
and the next man of your mind's pantheon

of redemption came to nuzzle and shuttle forth
metaphor into you until your rectum hurt,

that instead of sorrow you would find
the incomprehensibility of living in a hole.

*

Today's topic: everything
Tomorrow's topic: everything
The day after that's topic: everything

Intelligence shelved, is it the impulse
that validates itself?

*

The majordomo unleashes the radio
and would have us chug some coffee.

Gold leaf, gilt echo, through the window,
a goat nosing through the fog.

Under the art nouveau dome they've been
serving original cappuccino since 1927.

A waist, an apron, the serving gesture,
the gesture of setting down, a manner of thanking,

the gesture of tipping, the gesture of placing
coins on the eyes of the deceased.

Is familiarity still comforting
when what is familiar is

a misshapen breast and the heave
of *Carmina Burana?* She swears

she doesn't know the masked men
running around with Schiller's marble head.

Apparently *Mephisto* is
spumoni with amaretto

and we have sold our souls to this web of blue
Christmas tree lights.

There are gargoyles on the cistern
and maggots in the sugar,

but it's our conversation about the nature
of hate, and why we're sort of o.k. with it,

that makes me question, "Excuse me, Ma'am
could you possibly burn these napkins,

so I can watch them flutter up the flue
like all the devil's feathers?"

*

w wa wav wave wavel wavele wavelet avelet velet elet let et t

*

In the Turkish baths everyone in ones.
In the Turkish baths all of us pulling off

the loincloth look in cotton aprons.
The view from fabric shields equal

to the view from the interior of a TV—blur
of languor, black and white, throat-deep

in hot sulfuric water, weightless.
Toes break the surface, worthless

nuggets in steam. The penis waves
like an excommunicated anemone.

Along the entirety of the fault line, at least
cigarettes and asses retain a defining structure.

We're the end of the spokes. The pool has no axle.
To take the heat elsewhere, to focus

on the holes in the domed cupola
and how to get through into night.

As if any constellations were shaped like fruit.
As if constellations were an educated manner of the stars.

The question here is not whether we will or will
not inherit this Earth, it is what to do

with an Earth that has inherited us.
Break the surface of the water with the ear

and the crack of a knuckle is
electricity through a tickwire.

Lions and cherubs spit on necks.
White horseshoes, water scarves—

folding, folded—the easiest part
is the dead man's float.

In the sauna I notice my pulse
flicker in the arch of my foot.

It would be too beautiful to feel
all of our blood at once.

*

If memory is a stupid butterfly's overseas voyage, my butterfly of
you is a stupid blue morpho and the year is 1100, so the Earth
has a flatness, the sea an edge. My memory's thorax is composed
of equal parts you in your office, pinching my ear, saying "don't
freak out," you in the Marais, piercing a vein, freaking out, a dog
in a river, pine needles in June, loam, steam, a ladle, Saints
(Sebastian, Matthew), the United States Postal Service, a Cuban
pulled pork sandwich, a condom, laurel, vomit, and a rose.
Though my memory's wings beat with abandon, halving the dis-
tance to empathy, this sea is still Zeno's, its edge out of reach.

*

We found Billie Holiday and Louis

Armstrong on the paper place mat,
faces mangled by wineglasses.

I had to leave to shit and find *Peace*
scrawled sideways on the stall wall

      on Earth, of cake, of ass
      process, pipe, be unto you

The color of this brocade reminds one not
of a tennis ball exactly but of Boris Becker,

the force behind the color. In this fancy
light I don't blame the Russian

with a perfect slur and lazy eye
for the money chumped on the bill.

I don't blame the stripper
who spoke of young corn.

Good corn, young corn.

I don't blame the six women in blue muslin
dancing in a field or the man next to them

swatting at a butterfly with his cigar.

*

In the morning's vapor the off-leash
dog stops at the fountain, tongue out,

pants at the three bronze dogs, tongues out,
heads corroded to green, panting back.

*

The problem: there is a complex
of tufa caves beneath the castle,

a pattern of loose alluvial rock bored
into a labyrinth, and somehow we have

descended into it. No matter the dark
or torches, the wet walls smell

sweet of leaf rot and urine
mixed with apples at the early

stages of ferment. A smell like those trees
we could never find that each spring smelled

like an orgasm. Hands pressed to wall grit,
I sniff and remember there is melancholy

immediately after love, remember tiny antennas
tuned to all the small volcanoes I never want to erupt.

*

s   se   see   seei   seein   seeing r   seeing re   seeing red   red   ed   d

*

In constant fog the world *does* end
in all directions, and stepping forward

over cobblestones and cast-off plastics into the blurred
vicinity of that iron raven on the shoulder of that iron

poet only pushes the end of the world further,
the hole of visibility following the body like an aura

until it is impossible to recognize
even where we came from.

*

"On my way to the hovel
I met a man upon

A bridge
He tipped

His bowler an'
Drew his cane

We rubbed the statue
And cursed the fog

And in this riddle
We've said his name"

*

Warn the museum. Here is Salci's gamepiece,
its rabbit torn open. A long crimson rip

down natty fur. How many times must we say
Look, there is no heart therein. The heart is in der Klinik.

Warn the museum. The horse morphed
again into centaur at the village

blacksmith, hoof propped on the block,
arguing for a new shoe: *Listen, Welby, I ache.*

Warn the museum. I miss Judith with the just-fucked
expression on her face, always so tender and detached

holding Holofernes' severed head like a fruit basket,
several tendons twanging, blood-warm sword

resting on her aureole. Two women need no intervention
from God to kill a man. The maidservant gives

Holofernes a pile driver, the executioner
looks puzzled and pretty for the painter.

If the artist had more gall
he would ask them to wrap

the head in burlap
and throw it into the fog.

*

Recurring, the sad fact the knapsack's
much lighter on the shoulders when, cloud or no,
the *Iliad* you gave me is left repeatedly, inhospitably at the hotel.

*

The impatient blue
morpho is an unwelcome

web hog whose wings' miniscule scales
taste acidic from the leguminous

diet, yet he can't seem to wait
for the spider to gnaw him free.

He sheds iridescent
sequins onto the gluey

strands of the web,
flying out of skin.

We watch this, purposely ignoring
you on your deathbed in the Alps,

because we *have to,* because electricity is lolly-
gagging in your peculiar muscle caged by ribs.

Dear frayed rope of the aorta's footbridge,
piss off, we cough into the white. *Morpho,*

after all, is an epithet for Aphrodite,
your favorite goddess born of severed

genitals, born of lave and foam.
We could belabor love and rapture,

but the morpho's desire to molt is simply
yours to be here with me, possibly as a scruffy

Hungarian tobacconist with an ample heart
and a love of sweat, mine to be a crow over Budapest

with a nut in my beak
as the fog clots.

                    *

From the hole it is easy to feel more fully

outside, inside
a pocket of space with no hieratic
entwining of hours, location, the as-of-
yet unseen baby in Indiana already dribbling on
herself, as of tomato, of stone, the tornado that missed.

They are somewhere else.
They are all right here.

Here where we can kiss the sphinx so her stone hands on our spines
become paws, sprout claws, where we watch the Neanderthal blow flute.
The here of whirly bird, whirly bird, that was not a crow. Where with no

clock no
watch no
dial

        The only point of location is darkness.
        The only part left is to eye the cathedral,

        its spire residing on the other
        side of the mist like a periscope.

p   *pu*   *pul* *puls* *pulse* *ulse* *lse* *se* *e*

CONCUSSION

AILMENT

We tried splints. We tried steroid
injections, immobilization, oatmeal.
We tried ritual. We wrote Arabic
on our hands. We tried to understand.
Architecture we tried. We slid skylines
into the atmosphere like skeleton
keys. We tried buoys. *Buoy us,*
we pled. We tried pharmaceuticals.
Holler, restrain, holler. We tried lists.
We tried to be cognoscenti. Science,
we thought, we'll try science. Through
their middles we vivisected raccoons.
We tried penalties. We tried a feeling
of culpability. We waited. We waited
longer. We tried hyacinth, irony, snow.
We tried nosebleed. We tried to *flush
'em out.* We amounted to a scythe
swung at the public's endless, ambitious
weeds. We wrapped ourselves comically
around the ankles of those leaving us.
Red. We tried red. We tried red again.
We wouldn't renounce red. We rifled
through red's possessions. Riffed on it.
Red loam, red cosine, against red odds.
Variegated notions of red. We tried
appeasing red. *Buoy us, red. Bail us*

out. We bet on red. We voted for red.
We read red. We tried guilt. Gusto
we tried, and grew nostalgic for red.
We chewed betel leaves and rock salt.
Tenderness and resolution, both.
We placed our palms over our abdomens.
We tried abandonment. We absconded
with the buoys to look for red. We tried
valor. We were helmeted warriors. For
Hector we wept. We lurched. We tried
to *roil 'em, flush 'em out. Buoy us, bail us*
as we do this. We tried a cubic form.
We needed to *feel* this. We tried kudzu,
breast milk, we impaled. Tonguing, shrubs,
humiliation, sweat. We tried a lone
galvanized nail, protruding from a beam,
around which we hung ourselves like coats.

ASH WEDNESDAY

There is a starfish in my mussel.
There is a starfish marinated in my mussel shell and a bulldog
on the barstool. There is a French bulldog perched
like a sage before the Catholics'
table and the master Catholic's acolytes
are gawking at the bulldog with little charcoal
crucifixes scrawled across their foreheads to mark
the beginning of the season of lack.

There is a starfish in my fennel
wine sauce molded elliptically to the shape of the dark
elongated shell, one spiky limb limp
and tethered from the process of being
inadvertently served to the world.
There are the bulldog's wise, coruscating eyes
and there is the man's
voice in my ear rehashing the grisly deterioration of a former
partner. There is a star
beyond Sirius that is this man next to me: a ball of light in a Stereolab
T-shirt, the voice an uneasy equilibrium between the solar
energy of his nuclear fusion and his propensity to collapse midstory under
the weight of his own gravity.

As all things mammoth and behemoth end in a moth,
the beginning of hopelessness is always hope.
Our hope is not in the poem precisely, the hope is that the poem embodies

a hope for what it cannot accomplish. Over goblets of faux
Bordeaux we would sacrifice the body of any
text for an index of first lines,
those entry ribbons into
the laws of invisible things:

Tangerines and remorse;   217
The hypochondriac waiting with a punch   14
They gather in the saplings for a fire,   223
Truncated *Om* from   13

He fingers the starfish in my mussel and becomes
a black hole. Time becomes
a tuning fork he gongs on the counter and we slip
through a wormhole between prongs
to a velour disaster of a sofa from which
he points out over Stoli martinis up with a twist the painting
whose nebulous letter shapes refuse to coalesce into anything
resembling the word

"redemption."

We agreed the canvas was a hieroglyphic Ouija
board but couldn't decide
who was the Ouija master or whose hand went
on top. Redemption: to be
re-deemed, to be deemed
again, but what if we were deemed
worthless in the beginning?

If Berlin   188

If both breasts were of blown glass,   143

If not now, when shall the butterflies   130

If she hadn't born enough sons to bear her pall,   57

In a swathe of   140

Interior landscapes shall profess: 4

There is a starfish in my mussel and a bulldog in the narthex
of a church I don't know how to enter.
The light: puce. The score: one
death to zip. The world
becomes a series of strings and we run our fingers through the knots
looking for a way to unravel it.
If depression is a finger, and liberation is a finger, this disoriented *not
caring* is the tightening
fingercuffs between them. We are stuck here in the mild
concussion of living.

"I have begun to shower in the dark."

The starfish in my mussel is not the starfish on my beach
in Santa Cruz, where with two cronies, stoned, the hunt
was for seagulls and the tools our hands.
I was a bad stalker. I thought of scissors. Each of us was
drawn in sand, represented by an x,
the schematic of our strategy a Delphic triangle of how to kill
everything we loved using nothing
but flesh, wood, kelp.
I was trying to be a goldfish

because they have a memory
span of three seconds. My thoughts
were simple: Da Vinci invented scissors, I was born without kneecaps,
I am in my aquarium, I understand my fingers
in the runnels in the sand, but the rest of perception
is a codex of loose sheets and I am just
beginning to learn how to stab
bind. I was sewing a book to enter the world
when one of us noticed one of us
had wandered off into the sea and was standing knee-
deep in surf, covered with kelp, dripping
like a postmodern Proteus with a bandanna around his bicep and a
dead and mangled gull
hanging from his hand.

Yes, I	138
Yes, inferior to scarabs, the anxious ants	4
Yesterday's leaves will fall again	210
Your little eyes scouring outer space	84

There was a starfish in my runnel and one in my
mussel, a bulldog, the crucifix, the index,
there is a man in my ear and the death of his
lover, the imploding, the helix, the spume,
yet the harder we try to cultivate
a caustic view of humanity,
the more the birds fly in reverse
retracting the scars they've made in the sky.

No more irises	12
No more irises	12

HEMISPHERES

I split an orange and the day
fell in half.

On the counter—
ante meridiem hours, showers,

a lone green taxi and eggs, aspirin, chapters
of Leviticus and *The Economist,*

sly supermarket smiles, an appreciation
of dogwood, of ginkgo,

the employment pages—all lie
manifest in a ripe hemisphere.

From far below,
juicing on the floor,

I pick up the wedge
of twilight's slippery body,

pick up halter-tops and cocktail
lounges, sloe gin fizz,

pick up cicada whirr and elephant
grass, smog blocking the stars, tankers

dead in the harbor, pick up clubs
with men whose shirts say *J'adore Dior,*

pick up a breakdown,
still shaking in the street,

late-nite Lebanese
shawarma, burlesque, graffiti,

and heavy carnality, pick up a city
with a load of viscera roaming it.

I've been told to work
at reconciliation,

to synthesize, to live
only one life at a time,

so now I fit
the two halves of the sphere

back together and I think
they're right—the day

looks just lovely as a hummingbird
taut in the sun, hovering in chains.

MEKONG, MOHICAN

Lightning over the Mekong tonight—
lines down, lanterns up, iced
mulberry wine eddying
in a wineglass cracked as the Laotian
twilight, fractured though unbroken—
and I'm sensing total

blackout in Cleveland. My father's probably
driving north, white-knuckled,
parallel to the Mohican, magnetized
by the slow incantation of Jacob's Field,
threatening to *bitch-slap* the wayward
windshield wiper of the company pickup
and tuned-in to WQKT to see
if his one Indians game of the year's been called off.

Two monks stop at the table for a clandestine
English lesson in darkness; I start
with definitions less known—

father: *originator, founder, inventor, or*
the figure beneath the willow, casting corn cobs
to members of the Corvus family as alms.

son: *a male thought of as if in relation*
to a formative influence [a son of revolution].

riverbed: *the channel in which a river flows,*
or has flowed, or will flow toward the willow.

Gracious despite the logic of lost
metaphor, they invite me to a wat fortressed
by cobalt shadows and an alleyway of bells.
Third glass. Vision adjusted. Third inning—
a line drive ripped to deep left-center, a tight white ball
of sticky rice placed at the stone foot of Buddha.
High in the nosebleed section I hear
him drop the nachos, clap, and cuss
as if he'd just witnessed the failed
birth of his first and purple son.

sedentary: *not migratory, as some birds.*

Before lotus and incense, I kneel
to offer what I never fully gave
his willow—myself—and he stands
soaked, the spring-loaded stadium seat
bobbing in mockery, to watch the monstrous blue
tarpaulin being pulled over the diamond,
settling over the seventh inning
cancellation like a bad memory
of crows or the carpet bombing of Laos.

bedrock: *the solid rock beneath the soil and superficial rock.*

Obsidian outside the temple gate.
A father and son are selling sheaves
of Mekong seaweed by candlelight—
my father's face is illuminated
by the dome light as he pries open
the door to the pickup in the parking garage.
I buy two squares. Eat one.

dredge: *a net attached to a frame, dragged*
along the bottom of a river, a bay, a son, etc.
to gather shellfish, to gather years, to gather . . .

Southbound now in the downpour
he kills the radio's anarchic fuzz.
Almost bald enough, approaching
the willow, crows, Mohican again,
he scratches his leg in silence through
the folds of the monastic saffron robe.

SPUN

"... *into what would be the most shimmering, delicate thing*
in the world were it not for the spider in the corner"
—André Breton, *Nadja*

A mason in a pickup sees broken
bottle shards briefly
shimmer in his headlights at 5:00 a.m.—

accelerating, they become to him neon
beer signs refracted to confetti on the river;

accelerating, the lines on the road grow
smaller, the guardrail nearer, brighter, nearer;

"please pass the ammonia";

the sound of a kitchen knife zipping
down a synthetic cutting board
through a roma tomato and again;

the arc and flicker of the sun, the streetlamp, the surface of the brain;

is there ever an end to the impulse to assemble?;

they dip steamed artichoke leaves
into lemon butter, agree they're over-
cooked—neither eats the heart, never eat the heart;

"no, I guess I just wanted him to split me down the middle";

where the need to be wanted is a fact
worked into the psyche of the priest as he imagines
hands working pure aloe into his lesioned back—

he glances over his shoulder to see
the tips of her fingers
appear, disappear, appear;

a swarm of aphids overtakes an oak leaf;

a young mother with fasciitis feels
the membrane encasing her muscles
shrivel, become sand;

"take three at a time. Oooh.";

the mortician drops his cigarette onto a gladiolus
stalk, watches a small black halo develop;

where patterns of caramelized light frame a neglected rendezvous;

a cheerleader smears cortisone on her inner thigh,
refuses to tell her father the origin;

where confidence is a loose-fitting mural above our gist of fluidity;

"step on his tail and slide your hand up his back
  so he don't stab you again with his fin";

in the slaughterhouse the bleeder
slits the gullet of a heifer, hanging
from a cable around her ankle,

watches his hip-waders become
comfortably ensconced in the flow—
rigor mortis—he stares into her eyes;

"Who is this. What was that."

There is always someone else in the room.

LUCIAN THROUGH AN
ACHROMATIC LENS

if his name were just Lucian, she wouldn't be standing there like
that: too soon after, robe open, hair metaphysical, curvilinear ver-
tebrae, full-tilt breast: if his name were Lucian she wouldn't be
saying *you nimrod* as she watches his semen streak down the inte-
rior of her thigh, eclipse her knee: if his name were Lucian, he
would circle her: parallax: her freckles would resemble hand-
rolled tea buds: jasmine phoenix pearl: if his name were Lucian,
they would reach agreement on autumn: best season, beginning of
degeneration: if Lucian, larceny: they would find ample seagulls in
the parking lot of the landlocked shopping mall: filching M&M's
from tire treads: if his name were Lucian, she would face the win-
dow, point out the Anabaptist in a black bonnet in front of the
cigar shop: poking flowerpots with a Geiger counter: radiation,
radiate: if Lucian, comfortable in disjunction: he would be buried:
nostril-deep in the unidentified variety of hibiscus: as Lucian he
wouldn't flee his sentimentality: he would embrace his sentimen-
tality: then molest it: Lucian would be a veteran acrobat: acanthus
everywhere: Lucian, no more humiliation: Lucian, the space
between action and memory becoming negligible: an aloe leaf
oozing, a fist around an ice pick, paying dearly for its hubris:
Lucian: the glassy cornea your name: turned unprotected upon a
welder's arc:

JUNK SUITE

1.

Just east of a combine axing oilseed rape,
just west of Independence Day's
machine-gun fruit salad across the sky:
a river cutting a deep blue ribbon
through Wisconsin, the intricate
netting of a low-slung hammock, a mouse
carcass on the counter in lately-sprung trap,
then Psyche in the guise of a twilight moth
circling the stemware amid citronella
and Merlot, her uncertain relation to the system
of pine needles stuck to the bare soles of two men—
me on the mulch regarding you in the cabin,
withdrawing on the futon, your quadravision
weaving even your own virtues into polyhedrons,
until the landscape you see beyond
the unswept deck exists as its own sort of infinity,
eventually distilled into a simple chapel of gestures,
where you maintain that each touch of my palm
to bark to skin to a bottle to pull again and again
swigs from the fifth of whiskey is
mythological, where you see each amber blade of light
through the rack on the gas grill as
historical, where understanding is merely understanding
the equation of white bands that form on the skin

on the days our fingers cling to the hammock like talons,
is merely understanding the arc of the driftwood, thrown
repeatedly to a dog by a boy on the dock,
his cancer-laden flat-coated retriever now rising,
now falling, in a speedboat's ruthless wake.

2.

The mannequin's left arm parallel to the mannequin's
right; First Avenue perpendicular to First
Street; upstate, a stand of alpine pines all parallel to each
other and perpendicular to the long spines of their cones
on the ground; a row of cadets in the West Point
mess hall, parallel to a row of cadets in the West Point
mess hall, eating each forkful at ninety degrees; four feet
waltzing in boxes across the dim ballroom floor;
goalposts, flagpoles, mortar joints between the herringbone
pattern of bricks, a set of encyclopedias
on the bookshelf, stiff, leather and sustained
by the bookend reverse L and the bookend L;
a tatami mat rolled flat across the silent *ryokan;*
Second Avenue perpendicular to Second
Street; two parallel sticks of lit incense waved then stuck in
the cauldron of ash outside the temple to respect
the dead; two parallel chopsticks licked clean then stuck in
a bowl of jasmine rice on the table to disrespect
the dead; Third Avenue perpendicular to Third
Street; in the Upper East Side of the grid, the glass hotel's
floor upon floor upon floor, a hall, then a door, then a bed;

two bodies above the covers, head to toe to toe
to head, inches apart, swapping heat; one swivels his eyes
toward the window, watches the reflection of the other
grab the screwdriver from the drawer, carve slow red victory laps
around a nipple, then quietly wrap the tool in graph paper.

3.

In trouble, we scribbled indiscretions
across the implacable chalkboard:

I will not mention the century or motion toward heaven
I will not mention the century or motion toward
(heaven I will not mention)
the century or motion
toward heaven
I will
not mention the century or
motion toward
heave

4.

The riot of river water gone deep sepia from peat.
From above you swore you saw in the falls'
crash landing a portrait of Moses or Samothrace,
& I scanned the line of your bicep, past the gully
of flesh formerly reserved for skids, for self-

imposed postmodern stigmata, past fingers,
past cuticles, and lost my eyes
in the melee of swirls, where I swore I saw nothing
but a loose cyclone of foam opening like a portal
to the year before we came here, when you came here
to die. You failed. We do. You paddled
in a hijacked kayak past the beach's spherical stones,
that vermilion acre of bulbous caviar—though you had
seen them simpler: rotten peas, crab roe—far past
black boulders and golden lichen you'd taken
as your soul, past fat gulls and arctic ducks
into a girth of water too cold for faith,
toward the horizon line between lake and sky,
a line pulled taut by our peripheral gods, pulled
straighter than any needle, hypodermic or pine,
where you stopped, and flipped, and didn't
die but *departed* so methodically trying.

5.

I will not want.
I will not want.
I will not want.
I will no

6.

Piton, crampon, piton, crampon, ax.

Breath, pulse, pause, pulse, crevasse.

In the snowed-in sanatorium a range of lime
mountains floats across your heart monitor.

Here one of the clouds is shaped like an orphan
beneath which a scarecrow moves on its crucifix.

There is irony in getting sick as soon as you are fixed.

In the snowed-in sanatorium in the anesthetist's grip
you've begun to rappel beyond recoverable limits.

Here the orphan cloud has morphed
into an intern lubing your defibrillator.

Breath, pause, "clear," pulse, crevasse.

Piton, crampon, piton, crampon, ax.

QUANDARIES

Quandary

the figure has moved up the slope of the scape and lain
down on rock | igneous black | lacquered with wet | the figure has
reclined on a fissure in the jut before the blue | the blue moves
in | the blue moves out | beneath the fissure
in the rock is a depth | beneath the depth is the red
the red beneath the depth in the fissure will erupt
if the figure inclines | the figure a trigger | if the red erupts
the scape will dissolve | the figure will melt on the jut | a death |
if the figure remains reclined | the red will remain arrested
beneath the depth | beneath the fissure | beneath the figure | but
a figure reclined on a rock forever will weather until the figure dies |
the figure regards the sun | the figure regards the blue

The Figure Bleeds Twice

the figure discovers a clast
fractured from the shelf | the figure grasps
the clast between the figure's forefinger and the figure's
thumb | the figure casts the clast into the blue |
the blue goes down | the blue comes up | the blue moves in
ripples | the figure discovers another clast fractured from the shelf
the figure grasps the clast and presses the clast into the shelf |
the finger turns red | the rock turns red | the finger turns
numb | the figure rubs the finger against the thumb

thumb red | finger red | jut red above
the black | the figure regards the figure's self |
the figure discovers the figure's self
is also red below | the figure does not know
how to bleed | why to bleed | when to bleed
the figure only knows the bleeding
is good | the figure rubs the numb
forefinger and red thumb over the opposite
red of the figure's below | mix of reds | the blue
moves in | the blue moves out | the finger moves in |
the finger moves out | the figure threads opposite reds |
one of pain from the fractured clast | one preparation
for another figure to come | the figure regards the sun

Quandary

the soldier has wandered off into the green and lain
down on a plot | elephant grass | lacquered with wet | weapon on chest |
the soldier on the plot has reclined on a land mine | the elephant
grass moves left | the elephant
grass moves right | the land mine clicks but the river
retains its shape | beneath the weapon is the soldier |
beneath the soldier is the grass | inside the grass is the mine |
          beneath the mine
is the plot | if the soldier inclines the mine on the plot
will explode | the soldier a trigger | if the mine explodes
the grass will burst | bamboo will burst | the soldier's mind
will burst on the plot | a death |

if the soldier remains reclined on the elephant
grass the mine on the plot will remain
arrested | beneath the soldier | above the grass | above the plot | but
a soldier reclined on a plot forever will weather until the soldier dies |
the soldier regards the weapon | the soldier regards the plot

The Soldier Bleeds Twice

the soldier removes the soldier's hand from the soldier's lower
zone of wound | the bamboo leans in | the bamboo leans
out | the soldier arrests
the red of the wound with the butt
of the weapon | the red beneath the butt lacquers
the butt with itself | the soldier discovers and plucks a stalk
of reed from the plot of elephant
grass | the green
reminds the soldier of the mine below and the soldier's mind
retracts | the river retracts | the soldier retracts
the butt from the wound | the red drips but the river retains
its shape | the soldier lacerates
the soldier's forearm with the stalk to mark a rising
and a falling of the sun | the soldier refits the butt
into the lower zone of wound | a rising and a falling |
the soldier regards the blunt
edge of the butt | the soldier collates the days in red in rows
with the stalk across the forearm | the days are
eleven | the elephant
grass moves in waves until the soldier replaces

the butt with the collated forearm to plug
the lower zone of wound | the plot
does not know how to thicken but the river reminds the soldier of thirst |
the soldier thirsts and the elephant grass is no longer
lacquered with wet | the soldier resorts | the soldier licks
the butt of the weapon clear
clean of the soldier's inevitable red

Deus ex Ptero

imprisoned on the fissure the figure considers
the sun and the coming of a large-winged one |
the blue moves in | the blue moves
out | the figure has never encountered
a large-winged one | even the animal that slept with the figure is
not transmutable to wings | so the figure discovers
a clast fractured from the shelf | the figure grasps
the clast and draws a little new red from the fore-
finger | the figure traces the finger on the rock
in the shape of a large-winged one | the little large-
winged one dries | flaps | floats off the jut | off
into the blue between trees | the blue moves
in | the blue retracts | the trees sway in | the sun
retracts | the figure traces a larger large-winged one |
this one dries | this one lifts | this one floats over to an animal
and flaps an animal to death |
the figure stops creating |
the figure regards the scape |

Quandary

the grandmother has been rolled across the ward and lain
down on a cot | lacquered with sweat | the grandmother has
reclined on a cot before the family | the family moves
in | the family moves out | but the grandmother retains
her shape | the grandmother is in the shape of the spare
white space between the spoon and the phone
in the ward | beneath the grandmother is the sheet | beneath
the sheet is the cot | beneath the cot
is the plug | without the plug is the immediate
black | if the family inclines the years will suffice |
if the years suffice the grandmother will face
the immediate | a death |
the spoon is regarded | the phone is
regarded | if the family inclines the grandmother will remain
reclined in the ward | lacquered with sweat | the plug will remain arrested
beneath the cot | beneath the sheet | beneath the grandmother | but
a grandmother reclined on a cot forever will weather until the grand-
       mother dies |
the family regards the plug | the grandmother regards the blue

Deus ex Cutlery

imprisoned in the ether the grandmother considers
the coming of her lord and the coming of her
cutlery | the family

lopes in | the family lopes out | the niece
places the spoons from the ward on the sheet | lacquered
        with sweat | beneath
the sheet is the plug | above
the phone in the ward is the inclination
of her lord | from the ether the grandmother figures
psychokinesis into the niece's
spoons | the grandmother curls the spoons into the spare
white shape of the lord | real or imagined | reclined
on the cot the grandmother considers the lifting of the spoons | the spoons
lift | glint | hurl
through the ether across the ward | the grandmother is
reclined | the lord is | hurling
toward the phone on the wall of the ward above
the cot | the plug
buzzes | the family considers the black | the lord
crashes into the phone and falls completely
back into spoons | the niece
guards her mouth with her hand and regards
the floor | the cutlery shines | the phone
rings | and rings | and rings

The Soldier Considers Ranks

revulsed by the lower
zone of wound and the wind over the surfeit of elephant
grass the soldier casts
the weapon into the blue over the surface of the green | the butt

lands and the weapon fires
a shot over the plot | the soldier shudders and considers
the ranks | the ranks
are a facet of the soldier and the soldier
a facet of the ranks but do the ranks return
the soldier's regard | do the ranks now arrange
flowers into the shape of the soldier | does the river
remember the reflection of the ranks |
had the soldier not
inclined to wander off into the green and recline
on a land mine in the elephant
grass could the plot
have ever been different | had the soldier not
regarded the river | had the soldier
not mistaken the ranks for a facet
hidden within | had the soldier not
just cast the soldier's only companion | the weapon |
off into the green of the elephant grass on the plot | had the soldier
not

Quandary

the carpenter has moved up the slope of the roof and slapped
a sheet of plywood
down on the trusses | the carpenter trusts the trusses
and knows the trusses as ribs | the carpenter fits
the sheet into a pair of H-clips and regards
the cul-de-sac | the station

wagon moves in | the station wagon moves out | the pair
of H-clips resembles a pair
of H's and the carpenter refers
to carpenters as carps | the carp fires nails from the carp's
nail gun through the sheet | the nails
sail into trusses and the carp regards
the station wagon wheeling
around the cul-de-sac | the nail gun sails
an inadvertent nail through the steel of the carpenter's steel-
toed boot | the carp recoils and drops the carp's
box of chalk | the carpenters' toe
is nailed to the plywood | the plywood is nailed to the truss |
the carpenter cusses and regards the station
wagon in the cul-de-sac | the nail gun is dropped | the red
wells up in the boot | the carp reclines on the slope | the blue
moves above | the red blooms
below | if the carpenter rips the carpenter's toe
from the carpenter's boot the toe
will wither until the death of the toe | but a carpenter reclined
on a roof forever will weather until the carpenter dies | the carp
regards the cul-de-sac | the carp regards the sun

The Carpenter Considers the Stepson

crucified to the roof through the toe in the steel-toed boot the carp
reclines on the slope of the many-ply plywood and considers
the stepson | a station

wagon idles in the cul-de-sac | the carpenter remembers the
       stepson's bottle
rockets and grabs the nail gun | with the carpenter's forefinger and
       the carpenter's
thumb the carp peels
back the safety of the double-safety
nail gun | red creeps
from the boot up the ankle | the trusses bow
in | the trusses bow out | but
the cul-de-sac retains its shape | the carp
sails a nail up into the blue above the roof and refers to nails as bottle
rockets | the nail revolves
and makes a sound | the sound resembles the stepson
crying | the station wagon backfires and the carp regards a sheet of pink
styrofoam | the plies of the many-ply plywood are considered |
       the styrofoam is
considered | sending a message to the stepson is
considered | toward the knee the red creeps | the carpenter sails
a nail into the pink
sheet of styrofoam | the nail sticks | the carp retards
the safety of the double-safety nail gun with a strip of duct
tape and fires | and fires | and fires
nails into the pink of the pink
sheet of styrofoam | the station wagon starts back
up | the trusses
truss | the styrofoam is pierced in multiple and resembles
a message to the stepson |
ROBBY | ROBBY | ROBBY | SORRY

The Figure Considers Fossils

imprisoned on the fissure the figure considers
the fossils in the rock between the figure and the arrested
red | the arrested red is arrested beneath the depth
by the figure | but the fossils between
the figure's fissure and the arrested red
are not arrested | the fossils are rather a facet of the rock |
the rock is a facet of the slope | the slope is a facet of the jut | the jut
is a facet of the scape | the scape is a facet of creation | the figure figures
creation contains no large-winged ones | the large-winged ones
were either created by the figure's considerations
or have abandoned the figure altogether | either
way the figure's existence on the jut is the sum of the figure's actions |
the figure refuses despair | instead the figure regards
the trees on the lacquered black space
between the figure and the blue on the scape | the trees sway in
but the fossils retain their shape | the figure considers the fossils
individually | the figure experiences each fossil as the figure
would experience the figure were the figure regarding the figure
       from the other
side of the moving blue | layer by layer the figure considers
the shape of each fossil | the size of each fossil | the era of each |
the figure considers deeper and deeper through layers of creation |
until the figure arrives at the fossil of a gun

Deus ex Helicopter

imprisoned in the plot the soldier considers
the river and the coming of a helicopter | the bamboo moves
in | the bamboo moves out | the soldier remembers
a copter but has not encountered a copter
forever | the copter remembered was in the shape of the wet
green space between the soldier and the river on the plot |
the soldier discovers and plucks a stalk
of reed from the green on the plot | the soldier presses
the reed between the soldier's thumb and the soldier's other
thumb | the soldier blows through the stalk and the wind
blows across the plot | the stalk makes a sound | the sound resembles
a weapon but not a copter | the soldier resembles
a figure and discovers and plucks a larger reed from the plot | the river
retracts | lacquered with itself | the sun retracts | the soldier presses
the larger stalk between the soldier's thumb and other
thumb and blows | the sound becomes that of a copter |
the copter lifts | the copter floats across the green of the elephant
grass on the plot | floats over to an elephant
and slices an elephant to death |
the soldier stops creating |
the soldier regards the green |

The Watch

before the grandmother's cot in the ward the niece has knelt and been

abandoned by the family to keep

watch | the family sleeps | the niece keeps

watch | *Our Father, who art in* | a spoon in

the room beneath the phone catches and keeps the niece's

attention | the plug

buzzes but the grandmother's hands

retain their shape | with the niece's forefinger and the niece's

thumb the niece grabs the spoon and reclines

next to the grandmother | the sheet beneath

the grandmother and niece resembles a spare

white flower | to the grandmother's

face | lacquered with sweat | the spoon is

lifted | from the ether the grandmother

on the cot does not regard the opposite

grandmother contained in the implacable spoon |

regardless the niece keeps

and keeps | and keeps | watch |

reclined on the cot with the grandmother the niece

shivers and lifts

to the grandmother's chest a small

white flower | *Our Father*

The Silver

the soldier has moved the forearm across the chest and grasped
with the soldier's forefinger and the soldier's thumb the dog
tags | the soldier peers into the silver and the opposite
silver soldier leers at the soldier in the plot from the other
side of the implacable name | the name shines
in the sun but the soldier's face retains its shape |
the soldier in the plot extends the lips toward the opposite silver
soldier | the opposite silver soldier extends the lips toward
the soldier on the green | the lips and the lips meet in a kiss
across the soldier's name | the soldier closes the soldier's eyes and rolls
left into the green and the mine
erupts beneath the soldier | the wind stops | the plot
is lacquered with a big red flower |

The Blue

the figure has moved down the slope of the scape and peered
into the blue | the blue moves
in | the blue moves out | the opposite blue
figure leers at the figure on the scape from the other
side of the implacable blue | the opposite figure moves
in | the opposite figure moves out | the figure extends a forefinger
toward the opposite figure in the blue | the opposite figure extends
a forefinger toward the figure on the slope | forefingers touch in a ripple
and the figure becomes a flower |

COLOPHON

Forge was designed at Coffee House Press in the historic warehouse district of downtown Minneapolis. The text is set in Minion.

FUNDER ACKNOWLEDGMENTS

Coffee House Press is an independent nonprofit literary publisher. Our books are made possible through the generous support of grants and gifts from many foundations, corporate giving programs, individuals, and through state and federal support. This book received special project support from the Jerome Foundation, the Pacific Foundation, and the Witter Bynner Foundation. Coffee House Press receives general operating support from the Minnesota State Arts Board, through an appropriation by the Minnesota State Legislature and from the National Endowment for the Arts, a federal agency. Coffee House receives major funding from the McKnight Foundation, and from Target. Coffee House also receives significant support from: an anonymous donor; the Buuck Family Foundation; the Bush Foundation; the Patrick and Aimee Butler Family Foundation; Consortium Book Sales and Distribution; the Foundation for Contemporary Performance Arts; Stephen and Isabel Keating; the Outagamie Foundation; the law firm of Schwegman, Lundberg, Woessner & Kluth, P.A.; the James R. Thorpe Foundation; West Group; the Woessner Freeman Family Foundation; and many other generous individual donors.

To you and our many readers across the country, we send our thanks for your continuing support.

Good books are brewing at coffeehousepress.org